P9-ARZ-645

Revenge and Retribution

CRIME, JUSTICE, AND PUNISHMENT

Revenge and Retribution

Josh Wilker

Austin Sarat, GENERAL EDITOR

CHELSEA HOUSE PUBLISHERS
Philadelphia

*Frontis: At the funeral of a 15-year-old killed
in Bosnia.*

Chelsea House Publishers

Editor in Chief Stephen Reginald
Managing Editor James D. Gallager
Production Manager Pamela Loos
Art Director Sara Davis
Picture Editor Judy L. Hasday
Senior Production Editor Lisa Chippendale

Staff for REVENGE AND RETRIBUTION

Senior Editor John Ziff
Associate Art Director/Designer Takeshi Takahashi
Picture Researcher Gillian Speeth
Cover Illustration Takeshi Takahashi

© 1999 by Chelsea House Publishers, a subsidiary of
Haights Cross Communications. All rights reserved.
Printed and bound in the United States of America.

3 5 7 9 8 6 4 2

Library of Congress Cataloging-in-Publication Data

Wilker, Josh.
Revenge and Retribution / Josh Wilker; Austin Sarat, general editor.
    p.   cm. — (Crime, justice, and punishment)
Includes bibliographical references and index.
Summary: Uses literature and case studies to chronicle the
historic shift in the philosophy of punishing wrongdoers
and examines the continuing tension between the desire
for personal vengeance and public interest in lawfulness.

ISBN 0-7910-4321-5

1. Punishment—Juvenile literature. 2. Violent crimes—
Juvenile literature. 3. Criminal justice, Administration
of—Juvenile literature. 4. Revenge—Juvenile literature.
5. Revenge in literature—Juvenile literature. 6. Retribution—Juvenile literature. [1. Punishment. 2. Violent
crimes. 3. Criminal justice, Administration of. 4.
Revenge.] I. Sarat, Austin. II. Title. III. Series.
HV8693.W55 1998
364—dc21   97-47683
                                                   CIP
                                                   AC

Contents

CRIME, JUSTICE, AND PUNISHMENT

CAPITAL PUNISHMENT

CLASSIC CONS AND SWINDLES

DETECTIVES, PRIVATE EYES,
AND BOUNTY HUNTERS

THE FBI'S MOST WANTED

HATE CRIMES

INFAMOUS TRIALS

THE JURY

JUVENILE CRIME

PRISONS

RACE AND CRIME

REVENGE AND RETRIBUTION

RIGHTS OF THE ACCUSED

SERIAL MURDER

TERRORISM

VICTIMS AND VICTIMS' RIGHTS

WHITE-COLLAR CRIME

Fears and Fascinations:

An Introduction to Crime, Justice, and Punishment

By Austin Sarat

We live with crime and images of crime all around us. Crime evokes in most of us a deep aversion, a feeling of profound vulnerability, but it also evokes an equally deep fascination. Today, in major American cities the fear of crime is a major fact of life, some would say a disproportionate response to the realities of crime. Yet the fear of crime is real, palpable in the quickened steps and furtive glances of people walking down darkened streets. At the same time, we eagerly follow crime stories on television and in movies. We watch with a "who done it" curiosity, eager to see the illicit deed done, the investigation undertaken, the miscreant brought to justice and given his just deserts. On the streets the presence of crime is a reminder of our own vulnerability and the precariousness of our taken-for-granted rights and freedoms. On television and in the movies the crime story gives us a chance to probe our own darker motives, to ask "Is there a criminal within?" as well as to feel the collective satisfaction of seeing justice done.

Fear and fascination, these two poles of our engagement with crime, are, of course, only part of the story. Crime is, after all, a major social and legal problem, not just an issue of our individual psychology. Politicians today use our fear of, and fascination with, crime for political advantage. How we respond to crime, as well as to the political uses of the crime issue, tells us a lot about who we are as a people as well as what we value and what we tolerate. Is our response compassionate or severe? Do we seek to understand or to punish, to enact an angry vengeance or to rehabilitate and welcome the criminal back into our midst? The CRIME, JUSTICE, AND PUNISHMENT series is designed to explore these themes, to ask why we are fearful and fascinated, to probe the meanings and motivations of crimes and criminals and of our responses to them, and, finally, to ask what we can learn about ourselves and the society in which we live by examining our responses to crime.

Crime is always a challenge to the prevailing normative order and a test of the values and commitments of law-abiding people. It is sometimes a Raskolnikov-like act of defiance, an assertion of the unwillingness of some to live according to the rules of conduct laid out by organized society. In this sense, crime marks the limits of the law and reminds us of law's all-too-regular failures. Yet sometimes there is more desperation than defiance in criminal acts; sometimes they signal a deep pathology or need in the criminal. To confront crime is thus also to come face-to-face with the reality of social difference, of class privilege and extreme deprivation, of race and racism, of children neglected, abandoned, or abused whose response is to enact on others what they have experienced themselves. And occasionally crime, or what is labeled a criminal act, represents a call for justice, an appeal to a higher moral order against the inadequacies of existing law.

Figuring out the meaning of crime and the motivations of criminals and whether crime arises from defiance, desperation, or the appeal for justice is never an easy task. The motivations and meanings of crime are as varied as are the persons who engage in criminal conduct. They are as mysterious as any of the mysteries of the human soul. Yet the desire to know the secrets of crime and the criminal is a strong one, for in that knowledge may lie one step on the road to protection, if not an assurance of one's own personal safety. Nonetheless, as strong as that desire may be, there is no available technology that can allow us to know the whys of crime with much confidence, let alone a scientific certainty. We can, however, capture something about crime by studying the defiance, desperation, and quest for justice that may be associated with it. Books in the Crime, Justice, and Punishment series will take up that challenge. They tell stories of crime and criminals, some famous, most not, some glamorous and exciting, most mundane and commonplace.

This series will, in addition, take a sober look at American criminal justice, at the procedures through which we investigate crimes and identify criminals, at the institutions in which innocence or guilt is determined. In these procedures and institutions we confront the thrill of the chase as well as the challenge of protecting the rights of those who defy our laws. It is through the efficiency and dedication of law enforcement that we might capture the criminal; it is in the rare instances of their corruption or brutality that we feel perhaps our deepest betrayal. Police, prosecutors, defense lawyers, judges, and jurors administer criminal justice and in their daily actions give substance to the guarantees of the Bill of Rights. What is an adversarial system of justice? How does it work? Why do we have it? Books in the Crime, Justice, and Punishment series will examine the thrill of the chase as we seek to capture the criminal. They will also reveal the drama and majesty of the criminal trial as well as the day-to-day reality of a criminal justice system in which trials are the exception and negotiated pleas of guilty are the rule.

When the trial is over or the plea has been entered, when we have separated the innocent from the guilty, the moment of punishment has arrived. The injunction to punish the guilty, to respond to pain inflicted by inflicting pain, is as old as civilization itself. "An eye for an eye and a tooth for a tooth" is a biblical reminder that punishment must measure pain for pain. But our response to the criminal must be better than and different from the crime itself. The biblical admonition, along with the constitutional prohibition of "cruel and unusual punishment," signals that we seek to punish justly and to be just not only in the determination of who can and should be punished, but in how we punish as well. But neither reminder tells us what to do with the wrongdoer. Do we rape the rapist, or burn the home of the arsonist? Surely justice and decency say no. But, if not, then how can and should we punish? In a world in which punishment is neither identical to the crime nor an automatic response to it, choices must be made and we must make them. Books in the CRIME, JUSTICE, AND PUNISHMENT series will examine those choices and the practices, and politics, of punishment. How do we punish and why do we punish as we do? What can we learn about the rationality and appropriateness of today's responses to crime by examining our past and its responses? What works? Is there, and can there be, a just measure of pain?

CRIME, JUSTICE, AND PUNISHMENT brings together books on some of the great themes of human social life. The books in this series capture our fear and fascination with crime and examine our responses to it. They remind us of the deadly seriousness of these subjects. They bring together themes in law, literature, and popular culture to challenge us to think again, to think anew, about subjects that go to the heart of who we are and how we can and will live together.

*   *   *   *   *

Calls for vengeance today, as they always have, reverberate throughout society. These calls remind us of the tight link between anger and justice, between our sense of grievance over injuries inflicted and our desire to pay back injury with injury. In both ordinary and more celebrated cases victims now press for law to treat the criminal as he has treated them. Here and elsewhere a tide of resentment is rising against a system of public justice that allegedly appropriates and then silences the voice of the victim. The tendency of criminal justice systems in Western democracies is to displace the victim, to shut the door on those with the greatest interest in seeing justice done. In response, victims are demanding that their voices be heard throughout the criminal process. And in place after place their demands have been met.

The demand of victims for revenge recently has been vividly on display in the closely watched prosecutions of Timothy McVeigh and Terry Nichols for the bombing of the federal building in Oklahoma City. In those prosecutions reaction of survivors and the relatives of victims provided a crucial touchstone for evaluating the adequacy of the verdicts. Can and should law provide recognition of the pain of the victims of crime and cede power to them? Or, does doing so represent a regrettable return of revenge to the precincts of law from which it properly should be excluded?

These are the kinds of questions to which *Revenge and Retribution* speaks. By deftly combining historical material and contemporary case studies, this book shows us the pain to which law is asked to respond through its often technical, formal procedures. It takes us up close to cases from biblical times to the present, explaining how the desire for revenge both fuels and threatens legal justice. It asks its readers to think about some of the most important and difficult issues that law confronts through its engaging, yet rigorous, analysis.

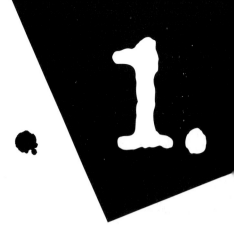

"HE JUST SNAPPED"

In the waning days of 1996, Leif O'Connel bought a wedding ring. It had been a good year, the best year of his life. He'd met a young woman named Annie Fulford. "In his mind," said Annie's mother, Carol, "she was the perfect woman."

O'Connel hadn't had much perfection in his life. The 23-year-old native of Mishawaka, Indiana, had grown up without a father. This absence ate away at him. After being a devout member of a church as a child, he dropped out at the age of 16. His mother said, "I guess he was disappointed God didn't answer his prayers. Leif always wanted a father."

He dropped out of high school too. He had trouble holding down jobs. His life tumbled forward, one imperfect situation giving way to another. But that was before he met Annie, before he fell in love, before he

Kary Holmes (right) wipes a tear from the eye of her mother, Carol Fulford, after the murder of Annie Fulford.

Lorna Hawkins, who lost two children to violence, produces and hosts Drive By Agony, *a cable TV show that seeks to help the loved ones of murder victims deal with their grief.*

caught sight of a perfect future, a future with someone to care for, someone who would care for him. Annie saw this future too. "She was so happy," said Carol Fulford. "She was so much in love."

On the night of December 27, 1996, not long after the couple had decided they would get married, Leif and Annie went to visit Annie's brother at his trailer home. They entered the trailer at approximately 10:00 P.M. Three strangers, demanding money and drugs, were holding Annie's brother and several of his friends at gunpoint.

O'Connel dug a can of Mace from his pocket and sprayed one of the gunmen in the eyes. A bad scene got worse—gunshots and screams rattled the walls. The gunmen ran. O'Connel looked for Annie. She lay on the ground, bleeding from a bullet wound in her head. She was rushed to a hospital, but within two hours the bullet had done its worst. She was gone.

For O'Connel, the future vanished. He saw only an unbroken string of poisoned days stretching out in front of him. "When Annie died," says Carol Fulford, "all he talked about was dying so he could be with her."

◆　　　◆　　　◆

Ours is not a perfect world. Too often the worst thing that could possibly happen, happens. More than 20,000 murders occur every year in the United States alone. Each one of these murders leaves in its wake an enormous amount of suffering and sorrow. Each one leaves behind people like Leif O'Connel, shattered by the loss of their piece of perfection.

"You never get past something like this," says a woman named Teresa Wheel, whose son was killed in a drive-by shooting. "It's a pain that reaches into the deepest part of your soul and tears you apart."

Joy Turner, another woman who lost her son to violent crime, says, "It's as if someone tore the roof off your house and snatched a part of you, and there's nothing you can do about it." The helplessness and grief that the loved ones of a murder victim feel sometimes make it seem that life is no longer worth living. Lorna Hawkins, who runs a cable television talk show devoted to helping the families of murder victims, says that many of the guests on her show "don't know what to do with their pain—they just say 'I want to die.'"

Leif O'Connel initially felt this kind of devastation. But his thoughts of suicide eventually gave way to another, more powerful desire. It was a kind of desire that all the loved ones of a murder victim, in every society since the dawn of civilization, have known in some shape or form. Leif O'Connel began to thirst for justice.

For some who lose a friend or family member to violent crime, this thirst does not deviate from a wish to see the murderers brought to justice in a lawful way, a wish to see the killers arrested by law enforcement agents, then proven guilty and sentenced for their crimes in a court of law.

But, in the United States, an increasing number of people do not believe that justice is adequately served in this way. The perception has grown in recent years that criminals do not have to pay any sort of meaningful price for their crimes. Excessively lenient jail sentences for violent offenders are now seen by many as the norm rather than the exception. According to a report released in August 1997 by The Urban Institute, this belief is not supported by fact. But, the report points out, "[p]ublic perceptions are driven by the sentencing for very serious offenses, particularly murder or homicide, and media reports of sentencing are most likely to focus on unusual and lenient sentences for violent offenders. Lighter sentences are more easily recalled in the public consciousness than are severe sentences, which are actually more common" (footnotes omitted). According to a recent survey, only 4 percent of Americans believe that convicted murderers will spend their lives in prison.

A woman named Emily Bryant, whose daughter Lisa was killed in 1993, says, "When you're a victim, there's almost no justice. Someone has lost a loved one, and this criminal is going to come back out, to get to laugh, be happy and carry on like everyone else, when he's taken a life? It doesn't make sense."

Emily's husband, Wilbert, a retired army colonel, takes this sense of injustice a step further. Speaking of his daughter's murderer, he says, "Even when I was in Vietnam, I didn't feel the rage for the Vietcong I feel for this man. I'm a nonviolent person, but this murder has turned me into someone I'm not. [They] better keep him locked up, because there are a lot of people who are angry at him."

Mr. Bryant's ominous words hint at a willingness to at least contemplate ignoring the boundaries of our society's criminal justice system, to go outside the law and take personal revenge against the murderer of a loved one. Such a willingness is not unknown in our society. As faith in our criminal justice system declines, instances of private revenge rise. It is the kind of untamed justice that, throughout human history, has been known to escalate violence, to turn one murder into a string of murders, each murder a payback for the previous one. It is the kind of untamed justice that has been known to rip a society apart. Societies, over the centuries, have tried to keep private revenge in check. But without a solid faith that the state is sufficiently repaying violent crime with just punishment, private revenge cannot be held back.

The Reverend Billy Kirk of the Greater St. John's Missionary Baptist Church makes a point during a meeting of community and religious leaders in South Bend, Indiana. The meeting was called to promote racial harmony and head off further revenge killings in the wake of Leif O'Connel's murder of Robert Wardlow.

◆　　　◆　　　◆

In the early days of 1997, Leif O'Connel bought a .380-caliber handgun. It had been a bad year already, the worst year of his life. Annie Fulford had been torn away from him forever. A desire had been growing inside him, spreading like a gasoline fire, burning away his thoughts of suicide and anything else in its path. The desire was this: someone is going to pay.

Like a gasoline fire, the impulse for revenge quickly ran out of control. Leif O'Connel became someone he wasn't. This kind of grim transformation, according to psychologist Karen Horney, who penned a groundbreaking study of revenge in the 1940s, goes hand in hand with the yen for payback. Wrote Horney, "Every vindictiveness damages the core of the whole being."

O'Connel had not been a violent person. And he had never, according to all those who knew him well, shown any kind of prejudice. "He always cared about people," said his mother, "and he isn't a racist." It seems that his desire to make someone pay changed all of that.

The gunmen responsible for Annie Fulford's death were African Americans. Police believe that O'Connel and an accomplice, Jarred Kahlenbeck, began driving around the predominantly black Northwest Side of nearby South Bend, Indiana. O'Connel carried his loaded .380 with him.

No one but O'Connel can say what his emotional state was in the predawn hours of February 12, 1997. Maybe he felt something like the traumatized Vietnam veteran who explained a binge of vandalism by saying, "I wanted someone to know how it felt to get your life smashed up for no reason. . . . I wanted to do something as violent and meaningless as what was done to me." Carol Fulford explained O'Connel's actions on that dark morning in South Bend a bit more succinctly: "I think he just reached the breaking point where he just snapped."

Police have strong physical evidence linking O'Connel to the crime committed on February 12 on the Northwest Side. They also have a confession from O'Connel. It seems his thirst for justice smoldered and festered, becoming the vilest kind of revenge. He wanted to pay back Annie's murder by killing a black man, any black man.

Twenty-year-old Robert Wardlow was walking the streets toward his home that morning. A car pulled up beside him. A window came down and a .380-caliber handgun unloaded several shots into his body, dropping him to the snow-covered sidewalk.

Wardlow had no connection whatsoever with the killing of Annie Fulford. He worked at a convention center and was planning to go to art school. His mother would say of him, "Robert was just a good boy. The people who killed him took away a kind, sweet person, and the world can't afford to lose too many of those."

Trying to control acts of vengeance like the one that Leif O'Connel apparently undertook on February 12, 1997, has been, throughout history, one of humanity's most difficult tasks. But the difficulty of the task has always been outweighed by its vital importance. It is a problem that must be dealt with if a society is to be one based on peace and rational justice rather than on wild emotions and a thirst for blood.

The importance of controlling vengeance was reaffirmed as the sun was rising on a new day in February in South Bend, as police found Robert Wardlow dead, blood from his wounds still leaking from his body, staining the snow.

BLOOD CRYING FROM THE GROUND

"**A** single deed of blood provokes an endless series of retaliations: a hideous orgy of revenge rages through the land, an orgy which no one may escape; for old men and women and children perish, whether one by one, or in a general massacre. It ends only when there is hardly anyone left to kill. . . ."

This passage is from a book by Hubert J. Treston on revenge in the ancient world. It depicts a kind of revenge known as blood-vengeance, which seems to have been, at the beginning of civilization, the sole form of justice. There were no courts of law, no judges, no juries. There was only a general unspoken agreement that any wrong done would be avenged by the victim of the wrongdoing or by a member of the victim's family. Blood-vengeance tended to perpetuate violence, because each act of revenge called out for another act of revenge to answer it. Treston's passage depicts a nightmarish world, yet it is a world not so far

A distraught woman hugs the grave marker of her son, who was killed in ethnic violence in Bosnia. Throughout much of history, a wrong done to a loved one cried out for revenge against the wrongdoer.

A scene from the Iliad, *Homer's epic poem about war and revenge.*

away from our own. To a person living in Robert Wardlow's neighborhood, or Annie Fulford and Leif O'Connel's neighborhood, Treston's grim primeval realm would seem all too near. It is the kind of nightmare that the people in those places are trying to wake from.

After the facts about Robert Wardlow's murder began to come to light, community leaders in South Bend organized a rally against violence and racial intolerance. It was feared that Leif O'Connel's act of wild vengeance would find a violent echo and that the chain of murders started on the night of December 27, 1996, in Michael Fulford's trailer home would continue.

Black and white community leaders prayed together at the rally for an end to the violence. Everyone at the rally, which was reported to be one of the largest integrated gatherings South Bend had ever seen, knew that the threat of violence still loomed. Revenge runs deep. Bubbling beneath all the prayers for peace was an angry desire for justice. This desire was put succinctly

2,500 years ago by the Greek dramatist Aeschylus in a way that makes it seem as if he were looking across the millennia directly at the body of Robert Wardlow in the snow. He wrote, "It is but law that when the red drops have been spilled upon the ground they cry aloud for fresh blood."

Those who gathered in South Bend had seen enough blood already. But the questions remained: Could their prayers keep a desire as old as human civilization itself at bay? How could the cry for fresh blood be silenced?

This last question has been asked for thousands of years. Although the answers have varied considerably from one culture to another, over the millennia societies' responses have gradually converged, signaling one of the most important developments in human civilization: the shift from justice based on revenge to justice based on retribution.

Revenge, the earliest and most elemental form of justice, is retaliation for a wrong done, typically by doing to the offender something similar to what the offender has done to the victim. Revenge is a private matter: the party wronged—whether it be the actual victim or the victim's relatives or friends—takes the responsibility for seeing that justice is done. For this reason, the penalty the wrongdoer faces is limited only by what the victim is willing and able to do in retaliation. Perhaps because victimization often produces rage or perhaps because victims have believed that a severe response might deter future victimization, revenge has historically tended to be disproportionate to the original offense.

Retribution, on the other hand, theoretically constitutes a more rational and measured response to crime because it takes responsibility for punishing wrongdoers out of the hands of the actual victims. Retribution is public rather than private justice: authorities mete out punishment to wrongdoers according—at least in mod-

Achilles drags the corpse of Hector before the walls of Troy. The Greek warrior "in rage visited indignity on Hector day after day," a gruesome revenge for Hector's slaying of Achilles' best friend, Patroklos.

ern times—to the rules of the society's legal system.

Despite their fundamental differences, revenge and retribution fulfill a similar, and vital, need in human societies—namely, restoring a sense of justice after a crime has been committed. As many experts have observed, the outrage people feel when someone has violated a rule of society is quelled only when the wrongdoer is punished. Retribution plays the additional role of preserving public order by precluding the need for victims to seek private justice.

Much has been learned about the earliest societies' attitudes toward revenge by studying the few isolated cultures that continued the ritual of blood-vengeance well into the 20th century. In these cultures, revenge was not something to be avoided. On the contrary, people who wanted to be considered honorable had to take revenge for a wrong done to them. There was no other alternative. Blood-vengeance was one and the same as justice, and it was also the primary way for a man to prove himself as a worthy member of the society.

But blood-vengeance took a savage toll. "My father's grandfather, my own two grandfathers, my father, and my uncle were killed, as though a dread curse lay upon them," said one member of a 20th-century society in Montenegro (Yugoslavia) where blood-vengeance ruled. "My father and his brother and my brothers were killed even though all of them yearned to die peacefully in their beds beside their wives. Generation after generation, and the bloody chain was not broken."

The chain was never broken because of the tendency, in blood-vengeance, to pay back one injury with an even greater injury. Thus even a transgression that involved no bloodshed—a theft, for example—might lead to a spiraling chain of retaliations that culminated in widespread slaughter. "Blood-vengeance is not a good thing," said a woman from Montenegro.

> For example if you have done something bad to me, I take vengeance; that means with us: whatever it is that you do bad to me, I'll do it back to you . . . even worse than you did to me. If you have struck me, gotten me into some trouble, stolen from me, lied to me, placed some blame on me, I will be looking to do something even worse to you.

The compulsion "to do something even worse" marked the earliest stages of human civilization's development. In one of the earliest and most enduring works of literature ever produced, the *Iliad*, traditionally ascribed to the blind poet Homer, this ferocious kind of revenge thrashes like a raging bull at the very center of the action.

The ancient Greek epic is set during the war between the Greeks and the Trojans, and it tells the tale of Achilles, the greatest of the Greek warriors. At the beginning of the poem, Achilles refuses to fight, wishing to punish the Greek king Agamemnon for not giving him the proper amount of respect. The Greek troops suffer greatly without Achilles, but the petulant soldier refuses to end his protest against Agamemnon. But then Achilles' best friend, Patroklos, dies at the hands of the Trojan warrior Hector.

Achilles knows he will die in battle if he fights at Troy; his mother, the goddess Thetis, has told him so. But a more powerful urge than self-preservation soon rises within him. Achilles wants revenge. "For I have no desire myself to live and remain among men," he says, "unless I may kill Hector first with my own spear."

In addition to killing Hector, Achilles pledges to slit the throats of 12 Trojan youths before Patroklos's funeral pyre to avenge his friend's death. Clearly, it is on Achilles' mind to "do something even worse" than what has been done to him. When Achilles goes into battle, he cuts down everyone in his path, ignoring any and all pleas for mercy. To one Trojan who begs for his life, he says, "Grief comes to all whose sons meet my anger."

Achilles eventually carves a bloody swath to Hector. As the two warriors are about to square off, Hector suggests that they make a pact agreeing that the winner of their battle return the body of the loser to the loser's family. Achilles replies,

> Hector, I'll have no talk of pacts with you. . . .
> As between men and lions there are none,
> no concord between wolves and sheep, but all
> hold one another hateful through and through,
> so there can be no courtesy between us,
> no sworn truce, till one of us is down
> and glutting with his blood the wargod Ares.

After driving his spear through Hector's neck, Achilles stands above the dying Trojan, who makes a final plea that his body not be defiled. But the plea falls upon deaf ears: "Would God my passion drove me," Achilles declares, "to slaughter you and eat you raw, you've caused / such agony to me!" He then continues his revenge by dragging the dead Trojan from the back

Cain stands over the body of his brother Abel, whom he has just murdered out of jealousy. In the Bible story, God warns off anyone considering taking revenge on Cain, indicating that the Israelites were searching for a way to end the practice of blood-vengeance.

of his chariot through the dust outside the city of Troy. Later he drags the corpse around the tomb of Patroklos. As Homer put it: "Achilles in rage visited indignity on Hector day after day. . . ."

Achilles treats the corpse so viciously that the Greek gods, gazing down on the world from their lofty perch on Mount Olympus, finally decide to step in and put a stop to it. In their estimation, Achilles has gone far enough. Hector's body is returned to his father in Troy. With this small, godly limitation put on Achilles' vengeance, the poem ends.

In the ancient world there were few limitations on revenge at all. Someone with the power of Achilles could generally do as he wished. The lack of limitations inevitably led to the kind of escalated payback Achilles was so adept at, and subsequently to the kind of sorrow that made the Montenegrin man quoted earlier characterize blood-vengeance as "a dread curse." But the conclusion of the *Iliad* shows that there was a desire in the ancient Greek world, however small, to put at least some boundaries on revenge.

Another ancient society that, like the Greeks, lived upon lands bordering the Mediterranean Sea also wished to tame vengeance's chaotic fire. In the ninth century B.C.—a century before Homer is thought to have compiled the *Iliad*—the oral mythology of a tribe known as the Israelites was first collected and set down on paper. The written epic, which exists today as the first books of the Bible, shows, among other things, a society struggling to rise above unlimited acts of vengeance.

The Israelites, like other ancient societies, initially practiced blood-vengeance. But one of the earliest stories in the Bible, that of Cain and Abel, contains evidence that the tribe was searching for a way to end blood-vengeance. As is common in Bible stories, the way that is being searched for is soon provided by the Almighty. In the story of Cain and Abel, God steps in and breaks the chain of violence.

The story begins with Cain, jealous of his brother's success, coaxing Abel out into the fields and killing him. God then says to Cain, "The voice of your brother's blood is crying to me from the ground" (Genesis 4:10). (All Bible quotes are from the Revised Standard version.)

Blood crying from the ground is a call for justice. In the ancient world this call for justice was one and the same with a call for blood-vengeance. But in the story of Cain and Abel a new kind of justice emerges. God does not kill Cain but banishes him from the society, saying, "You shall be a fugitive and a wanderer on the earth" (Genesis 4:12).

"I shall be a fugitive and a wanderer on the earth," Cain laments, "and whoever finds me will slay me" (Genesis 4:14). Cain believes that the practice of blood-vengeance dooms him, that he will be hunted down and killed in retaliation for his murder of Abel. However, God puts a mark on Cain that will warn any-one away from exacting private revenge on him. More than mercy for Cain, God's actions give a clear message to his people: blood-vengeance will not be tolerated. "If any one slays Cain," God warns, "vengeance shall be taken on him sevenfold" (Genesis 4:15). In other words, any act of human revenge will meet with a ter-rible divine response.

3.

"And God Answered Him in Thunder"

The Israelites were not the only ancient society to have a god directing them away from taking private vengeance. In the early days of human civilization, the way toward transcending blood-vengeance, toward waking from that nightmare of blood and continuous bereavement, seemed always to come from heaven.

Around the middle of the 18th century B.C., in ancient Babylonia, a king named Hammurabi claimed that his culture's most powerful deity, the sun god Shamesh, had communicated to him a code of law for all Babylonians to follow. A seven-foot-tall stela, or stone slab, upon which the laws were inscribed exists to this day (it is at the Louvre Museum in Paris), as do contemporaneous fragments of the code and later copies. To a modern observer, the laws Hammurabi received from Shamesh seem excessively harsh. Twenty-seven separate crimes are listed that call for the criminal to be put to death, and several other crimes call for severe torture or even dismemberment. "If a son has struck his father," reads a typical directive, "they shall cut off his hand."

At the time of its creation, however, the Code of Hammurabi actually constituted a step forward in the taming of the wild justice of revenge. For, despite its harshness, the code—which in reality wasn't a systematic statement of Babylonian law so much as a sampling of legal decisions—represented an early experiment in retributive justice. Previously, it seems, only offenses against the gods or the king were considered crimes against the public order; all other transgressions, including theft, assault, and murder, were private matters to be settled privately. And that, of course, generally meant revenge. But the Code of Hammurabi forbade private acts of vengeance. It also outlawed monetary settlements between the criminal and the injured party. This type of settlement, called restitution, had been, like blood-vengeance, a much-used, private way for conflicts to be resolved. In fact, the Code of Hammurabi sternly avoided any kind of private resolution. It seems that Hammurabi, or the sun god who inspired him, had learned that private acts of vengeance and restitution can't put a conflict to rest.

Only by public action can a crime be punished with any kind of finality. In public retribution, the roiling emotions and the cries for blood sounding from the victims and their families are taken out of the center of the process. The Code of Hammurabi sought to restrain the limitless revenge that these emotions sparked and that had repeatedly marred earlier societies. And the code gave birth to the kind of state-controlled public retribution that would become a fundamental principle in all later codes of law.

In the Code of Hammurabi there is evidence of a belief that emerged gradually in the ancient world. This belief was that a crime not only harmed the victim and the victim's family, but it also damaged the

This stela from around the 18th century B.C. contains the Code of Hammurabi. The figures at the top represent Hammurabi, king of Babylon, and a god. Carved below are the code's 282 laws.

entire society. This belief underpins all retributive systems of justice.

Although various offenses might provoke vengeance from victims or qualify for retribution from society, murder, for reasons that are obvious, was regarded as a special problem. The Babylonians—and the Israelites, who produced the story of Cain and Abel—sensed that on some level murder affected everyone; it polluted all of society. (This belief has come to be known as the pollution doctrine.) More importantly, they sensed that an act of private vengeance would not remove the pollution but would only call out for another act of vengeance that would further injure society.

A few centuries after Hammurabi carved his laws into stone, the God who had exiled Cain delivered his own code of laws to the Israelites. It happened around the turn of the 13th century B.C. Moses had led his people out of slavery in Egypt, and three months into their journey they had come to the wilderness of Sinai. The book of the Bible titled Exodus states that thunder rumbled and lightning flashed above the itinerant tribe on their third day in the wilderness, and there came, from out of nowhere, a trumpet blast so loud that everyone trembled:

> And Mount Sinai was wrapped in smoke, because the LORD descended upon it in fire; and the smoke of it went up like the smoke of a kiln, and the whole mountain quaked greatly. And as the sound of the trumpet grew louder and louder, Moses spoke, and God answered him in thunder. (Exodus 19:18–19)

According to the Bible story, the thunderous voice of God then spelled out to Moses a lengthy code of laws, which the tribal leader in turn delivered to his people. The Ten Commandments, which defined the basic duties of the tribe to their God and to one another, formed the foundation of the code. Other laws followed the Ten Commandments, many of which may today seem arcane and unimportant. But running through the entire code—through laws as general as "Thou shalt not kill," and as specific as the one telling what to do when one man digs a pit and another man's ox falls in and gets hurt—is the feeling of a society struggling to find a way to live together peacefully. It is this feeling that would make the code, in its entirety, into one of the major landmarks in human history. The

thunder on Mount Sinai can still be heard echoing to this day.

One of the most influential facets of the Israelite code of laws was that it put strict limitations on private revenge. Like Hammurabi's code before it, the code generally seems to modern readers to be unduly severe. At one point the code states, "you shall give life for life, eye for eye, tooth for tooth, hand for hand, foot for foot, burn for burn, wound for wound, stripe for stripe" (Exodus 21:23–25). This principle of repaying injuries exactly—known as *lex talionis*—was set into law at that time not out of cruelty. On the contrary, *lex talionis* originated as a way to limit the human impulse to exact a revenge that exceeded the initial injury. In previous societies, where blood-vengeance predominat-

Although the Israelites strove to control revenge within their tribe, they believed that they were the instrument for enacting God's vengeance upon other peoples. Here the Israelites massacre their enemies the Canaanites.

ed, it was not an eye for an eye but more like 10 eyes for an eye.

The Israelites, at this stage in their history, were struggling for their very survival. They simply could not allow themselves to be ripped apart from within by the natural escalation of private acts of vengeance. Throughout the pages of the Old Testament, there is a sense that vengeance is an elemental force that must be kept in check within the society.

On the other hand, this elemental force could be set loose with impunity on other competing tribes. The early stories of Moses' tribe contain a kind of double-sided attitude toward vengeance. Unlimited vengeance on outsiders was allowed.

God promised vengeance against the unrighteous (the unrighteous being, basically, any person or tribe who threatened to do the tribe of Israel harm). "Vengeance is mine," God said, "and recompense, for the time when their foot shall slip; for the day of their calamity is at hand, and their doom comes swiftly" (Deuteronomy 32:35).

A belief that God would avenge the injustices that the Israelites had to endure as they were struggling for survival bonded the tribe together. And a belief that their suffering would be avenged buoyed them: "The righteous will rejoice when he sees the vengeance; he will bathe his feet in the blood of the wicked. Men will say, 'Surely there is a reward for the righteous; surely there is a God who judges on earth'" (Psalms 58:10–11).

A belief that God would exact vengeance did not exist long as merely a belief. It became action, and the so-called vengeance of God translated into bloodletting of massive proportions. In one instance, God said to Moses, "Avenge the people of Israel on the Midianites" (Numbers 31:2). Some of the Israelite men had, the Bible mentions earlier, slept with Midianite women and subsequently worshiped Midianite gods (Numbers 25:1–3). For this the Israelites had been punished with a plague. Then Moses set about making his tribe the instrument of the Lord's vengeance against the Midianites, carrying out the task with a ferocity that equaled or perhaps even exceeded that of Achilles.

After the Israelites slew all the Midianite soldiers, Moses ordered them to slaughter every male child and every woman who had had sexual intercourse in the Midianite tribe (Numbers 31:17–18).

"Calm This Black and Swelling Wrath"

With her lover Aegisthus, Clytemnestra prepares to kill her husband, Agamemnon. That murder, and the revenge killings that follow, motivate the action of the Oresteia, *the trilogy of plays by the Greek dramatist Aeschylus that explore the destructiveness of blood-vengeance.*

In 490 B.C., a king named Darius I, ruler of the powerful Persian Empire, dispatched a large force of soldiers to Greece. The king had vengeance on his mind.

For more than 200 years, Persian tyrants had been exerting control over Greek cities along the west coast of Asia Minor in what is today Turkey. When, beginning in 499 B.C., several of these cities revolted against Persian rule, the Greek city of Athens sent a token force to aid its brethren across the Aegean Sea. The Greeks stung the king's soldiers in a small battle at the city of Sardis. "Who are the Athenians?" Darius roared, shocked that anyone would dare to oppose him. But in the end, the Greeks proved no match for the mighty Persian Empire. After putting down the revolt in Asia Minor by 494 B.C., Darius began making plans to repay the challenge to his power with an overwhelming show of force in Greece itself.

The Persian army that invaded Greece in 490 far

outnumbered the Athenians when the two sides clashed on the Plain of Marathon. It appeared certain that a vengeful slaughter would occur. But it didn't. "Mere numbers were powerless against the spirit of free men fighting to defend their freedom," wrote Edith Hamilton of the battle in her book *The Greek Way*. "Liberty proved her power. A wave of exultant courage and faith swept through the city, and Athens started on her career."

A generation earlier Athenians had begun embracing a new form of government: democracy. Now their stunning defeat of the Persians seemed to confirm the wisdom of granting each citizen a say in how issues of government should be resolved, and Athens continued its groundbreaking experiment in government by the people and for the people.

Unbounded optimism and fearlessness urged the Athenians on in the earliest days of this democracy. They believed that by working together they could solve all of the problems that had haunted earlier societies. In their desire to find out how to build a peaceful and cohesive society, they did not turn away from any dilemma, no matter how thorny. "One problem, therefore, occupied their minds insistently," writes Greek scholar Philip Vellacott. "What is justice? What is the relationship of justice to vengeance?"

One of the boldest investigations of the concept of revenge ever undertaken, before or since, came from a soldier who had fought at the Battle of Marathon. This former warrior, named Aeschylus (525–456 B.C.), wrote a trio of plays known as the *Oresteia*, in which he depicted with unprecedented clarity both the emotions that fuel acts of vengeance and the vast wreckage these acts can leave behind.

The *Oresteia* tells the story of a royal family suffering mightily from the curse of blood-vengeance. At the time Aeschylus wrote the plays, Greek society was very much divided in its opinion of blood-vengeance. The

belief existed that crime should be punished publicly, by the whole society. But there also was a widespread sentiment that private acts of vengeance, especially in cases of homicide, were both noble and just. Aeschylus strove to resolve these conflicting opinions as he told of the cursed family of a young man named Orestes.

The first play in the trilogy, *Agamemnon*, opens with the return of the title character from the long and bitter Trojan War. Shortly after arriving in his kingdom in the Greek city-state of Argos, Agamemnon, the father of Orestes, is killed by his wife, Clytemnestra, and her lover, Aegisthus. For both killers, the murder is an act of vengeance. Clytemnestra blames her husband for the death of her youngest daughter, Iphigenia (in the version of the legend Aeschylus used, Agamemnon had sacrificed Iphigenia before the Trojan War so that the goddess Artemis would grant the Greek fleet, which Agamemnon commanded, favorable winds to sail to Troy). After murdering her husband, Clytemnes-

In 490 B.C., Athens decisively defeated the Persian army of King Darius I at the Battle of Marathon. During the wave of optimism that followed, the Athenians attempted to set up legal institutions that would solve forever the problem of blood-vengeance.

tra declares that "he, marked with his daughter's blood, was ripe for punishment." Aegisthus agrees that Agamemnon deserved to die, but his desire for vengeance has its roots in the previous generation: Agamemnon's father, Atreus, and Aegisthus's father, Thyestes, were brothers who had quarreled. Pretending to reconcile, Atreus had invited Thyestes and his sons to a feast, murdered all the boys except Aegisthus, and tricked Thyestes into eating his sons' flesh by disguising it in the food. "Thus satisfied, I could die now," says Aegisthus after the corpse of the king has been found, "seeing Agamemnon in the trap of Justice, dead."

The chain of vengeful murders continues in the second play, the *Choephori* (The Libation Bearers). The god Apollo commands that Orestes exact revenge for his father's murder by killing the killers. Apollo says to him, "Shed blood for blood."

Orestes believes that justice needs to be done, and he believes that he, as the son of Agamemnon, is the one to do it. He kills Aegisthus, but just before he completes his act of vengeance by murdering Clytemnestra, his mother pleads, "Down with your sword, my son! My own child, see this breast: here often your head lay, in sleep, while your soft mouth sucked from me the good milk that gave you life and strength."

Orestes wavers momentarily, admitting, "To kill a mother is terrible," but he is convinced by his friend Pylades to do what Apollo commanded. Soon after the murder, Orestes is haunted by invisible demons, "avenging hounds incensed by a mother's blood." These are the Furies, the avenging deities who in Greek mythology torment criminals. The play ends with Orestes, half mad, fleeing in terror from these spirits. The people of Argos, represented in the play by the Chorus, have the final word. They ask:

> When shall be solved this long feud's argument?
> When shall the ancestral curse relent,
> and sink to rest, its fury spent?

Statue of Athena, the Greek goddess of wisdom. In the Eumenides, *the final play of Aeschylus's* Oresteia, *Athena resolves the problem of unfettered revenge by articulating a place for vengeance within a rational, retributive system of justice.*

Aeschylus was asking this question himself, his mind not only on the blood-marred family of Agamemnon but on the entire practice of blood-vengeance itself. He showed, in the first two plays, how an admirable desire to see justice done can lead, in blood-vengeance, to a never-ending chain reaction of murder. In the final play, the *Eumenides* (The Kindly Ones), he points toward another way to obtain justice.

In that play, the gods intervene to help decide the fate of Orestes, who by this time has fled to Athens. The goddess of wisdom, Athena, speaks the message that Aeschylus wishes to convey, saying, "This is too

The Greek playwright Euripides. Like the older Aeschylus, he examined the problem of revenge through the story of Orestes. Unlike Aeschylus, however, he doubted that the Athenian democracy could overcome the primal pull of blood-vengeance.

grave a cause for any man to judge." Aeschylus is not saying by this that he believes we are better off putting our fates in the hands of the gods. He is saying that a case like that of Orestes cannot be decided by any one person alone, but by all citizens of a society working together. The proper place of vengeance in society will only be decided by that new Athenian invention: democracy.

In the play, the Chorus, which consists of the mythical Furies, wants Orestes to be killed. But Athena intervenes, arguing that condemning him without a "fair trial" would be nothing more than another one-sided act of punishment, like the chain of murders. The goddess leads in 12 citizens to hear the case and to decide Orestes' fate (Athens had also pioneered the citizens jury). At the conclusion of the trial, the citizens vote on whether Orestes should live or die. The vote is a tie. Athena breaks the tie, choosing life. The Furies protest, voicing the age-old desire for blood to be repaid by blood.

The final dialogue in the play is between Athena and the Furies. It is a coming together of the new ways and the old, the new ways being democracy, rational discussion, and public justice and the old ways being the wild, private justice of blood-vengeance. Aeschylus knows that the thirst for justice that resided in the old ways must not be lost, but it must be tamed. A world must be created in which citizens work together to find justice, instead of warring upon one another endlessly.

Aeschylus believed that he was living at the time and place where such an ideal world would come into existence. "Calm this black and swelling wrath," his goddess of wisdom says to those still thirsting for blood. "Honor and dignity await you: share with me a home in

Athens." By getting the Furies (now the Eumenides, or Kindly Ones, of the play's title) to give up their implacable quest for blood and to agree to live in Athens, Athena has in essence solved the problem of revenge. What Aeschylus is saying is this: the spirit of vengeance embodied by the Furies must be kept, or there can be no justice. But that spirit must be put at the service of a rational, measured, public retribution.

The Athenian democracy did not last long. Aeschylus would die before his beloved world crumbled, but another, younger Athenian dramatist, Euripides (ca. 484–406 B.C.), would be around to witness its demise. Euripides also brought his prodigious talents to bear on the subject of revenge, and his vantage point in history darkened his vision of the future.

In 431, war broke out between Athens, which by this time was a bona fide empire, and the other major Greek power, Sparta. The Pelopponesian War, as the conflict is called, would pit these two states and their allies against one another for more than 25 years before culminating in the total defeat of Athens in 404. Although Euripides didn't witness that event, he did see Athens slide back toward the kind of brutal practices it had briefly transcended. For example, when the independent island state of Melos refused to join the Athenian Empire, the citizens of Athens voted to exact a terrible punishment. In 416 the Athenians slaughtered every man on Melos and sold the women and children into slavery. Unlike the sunny world of rational justice and civility that Aeschylus had foreseen, Euripides glimpsed a future in which revenge ran wild.

His version of the story of Orestes, written around 408 B.C., is almost completely absent of the gods that populate Aeschylus's trilogy. Euripides recognized even more than Aeschylus that human beings determined their own destiny. Thus the Orestes that Euripides created kills his own mother not chiefly because Apollo suggests it, but because he believes it is the right thing to do. And this Orestes, without a god to blame for his actions, suffers even more than the character in Aeschylus's drama.

Early in the play, Agamemnon's brother Menelaus sees that Orestes looks as lifeless as a corpse and asks him, "What is the disease that ravages you?" Orestes replies, "Conscience. I recognize the horror of what I did."

Later he says, "I know I am a polluted man—I killed my mother. But that is not the sole truth. I avenged my father; and for that act I am pure." Orestes, in Euripides' masterful hands, comes to embody the violent contradiction at the very heart of private revenge. His torn mind contains the bloodthirsty ways of old along with the idea that such ways can't possibly be right.

The father of Clytemnestra, Tyndareos, gives a long and eloquent speech that points to a way in which society could rise above blood-vengeance. He lists the chain of vengeance that has led to the murder of his daughter and asks, "Where will you set the bound to misery?"

He goes on to say, "Our ancestors established a sound principle: The man guilty of murder they forbade to intrude on sight or presence of the citizens; his crime must be atoned by exile, not blood for blood; otherwise always one man's lot is to be involved with murder. . . ."

Tyndareos is unable to match his words with actions, however. Instead, the powerful elder lets his own emotions run wild. After all his lofty talk, he ends up wanting Orestes to pay for his daughter's murder with his life. Tyndareos does not take private vengeance; rather, he uses his extensive political influence to bully a council of citizens into the decision that Orestes will be stoned to death.

The character of Tyndareos expresses a failure in Athenian society to match lofty ideals with appropriate action. Ultimately the ideal of rational public retribution had failed to be sustained. Instead, powerful men had found ways to use the system to settle scores, to take their own private revenge on their enemies. Discussing this time, the Greek historian Thucydides wrote that "men tried to surpass all records by the ingenuity of their plots and the enormity of their revenges." Even democracy itself was sabotaged by a coup in 411.

The insanity of such a world is reflected by Orestes as the play nears its conclusion. Any kind of reason or desire for justice has vanished from Orestes' feverish mind. He says only this: "I want to hurt my enemies before I die, to pay back those who have betrayed me in their own coin, and hear them howling who brought misery on me."

At the end of the play, Orestes is on the brink of capping a spree of vengeful murders by setting his father's regal castle on fire. Apollo materializes from above to put an end to such a plan, but his presence is so flimsy it borders on a joke. Euripides seems to have suspected that the gods no longer had much significant influence on the world. Human beings were on their own, untamed revenge once again like a flaming torch in their hands. One false move and they could burn their own castle to the ground.

DIVINE VENGEANCE

The golden age of democracy in Athens lasted only a century, from 508 to 404 B.C. But civilization's long struggle to control the fire of revenge did not cease. About 400 years after the demise of Athens, a voice would implore humankind to put down the blazing torch it held in its hands.

The voice belonged to a man from the same tribe that Moses had led out of bondage in Egypt 1,300 years before. He had a message for the world. He scaled a mountain in the land of Galilee, and when a crowd followed him up the mountain, Jesus Christ preached to them what is today called the Sermon on the Mount. He told his listeners this:

> You have heard that it was said, "An eye for an eye and a tooth for a tooth." But I say to you, Do not resist one who is evil. But if anyone strikes you on the right cheek, turn to him the other also. (Matthew 5:38–39)

These words were nothing short of revolutionary: the utter transcendence of vengeful urges had never before been considered. Even in the many ancient cultures that had slowly and haltingly been limiting private revenge, no one had ever suggested that retribution be tossed away completely. To the Athenians, for example, this would have been an assault on justice itself.

It is likely that those who heard the Sermon on the Mount found Jesus' instructions to "turn the other cheek" difficult to follow, perhaps even a little baffling. After all, how could a person—or, by implication, a society—offer no resistance to, and exact no punishment from, wrongdoers? Were people to allow themselves to be robbed, raped, even murdered? Wouldn't that be a recipe for victimization of the innocent and domination by the evil in society?

Later scholars too have debated the meaning of Jesus' words. Many have suggested that he never intended them to be taken literally. Earlier in the Sermon on the Mount, for example, Jesus had given the following advice about avoiding adultery:

> But I say to you that everyone who looks lustfully at a woman has already committed adultery with her in his heart. If your right eye is your trouble, pluck it out and throw it away! . . . Again, if your right hand is your trouble, cut it off and throw it away; it is better that you lose one member than that your whole body go into hell. (Matthew 5:28–30)

Most Bible scholars agree that Jesus wasn't really advocating self-mutilation as a way to avoid adultery. What, then, was he driving at when he spoke about plucking out eyes and turning the other cheek? Commentators have offered various explanations. Some have speculated that Jesus used hyperbole to get his listeners' attention and to emphasize the need to avoid sin at all costs. Others feel that he was articulating a higher standard, one that people probably couldn't attain but that nonetheless pointed them toward God's will. "In a word," Jesus said, "you must be made perfect as your heavenly Father is perfect" (Matthew 5:48).

Whatever the case, Jesus' words changed the idea of the vengeance of God and created a new ideal for his followers. Previously, in the days of Moses, the vengeance of God was something that could be helped along by the swords of the Israelite soldiers. When God, in the Old Testament, says, "Vengeance is mine," it is said as a warning to all tribes who might oppose the Israelites.

But this vitally important phrase changes meaning as Jesus spells out his vision to the world. In one New Testament story, an adulteress is about to be stoned to death and Jesus intervenes. He says to all those on the brink of exacting their brutal retribution: "Let him who is without sin among you be the first to throw a stone at her" (John 8:7). Jesus believed that only God has the right to vengeance.

"If anyone strikes you on the right cheek, turn to him the other also," Jesus, depicted here preaching to a small crowd, urged. His suggestion that all vengeful desires should be transcended was revolutionary.

The Israelites had believed that God was the ultimate judge of earthly doings, but they saw that they also played a role in the dispensing of justice. As a society, they believed, they enacted retribution on the part of God. Jesus objected to this. He held that there should be no earthly vengeance at all.

The phrase "Vengeance is mine" shows up again in the New Testament, in Romans, a book authored by the apostle Paul. The meaning of the phrase has changed. Paul writes, "Beloved, never avenge yourselves, but leave it to the wrath of God; for it is written, 'Vengeance is mine, I will repay, says the Lord'" (Romans 12:19).

Jesus Christ's message, perhaps because it was a dream of such utter perfection, quickly attracted many followers, and Christianity grew into a powerful political entity. But also, perhaps, because it was a dream of such utter perfection, neither the Christian Church as a whole nor its individual members always heeded Jesus' message. Jesus had denounced vengeful urges, believing that revenge is a sin. But all too frequently, Christians—as the Israelites had done before them—slaughtered the enemies of their faith, all the while professing to be enacting the vengeance of God. Jews, for example, were blamed for the death of Christ, and so Christians periodically murdered Jews in organized massacres called pogroms. Divine vengeance, throughout history, has been a kind of blinder to put over one's eyes. The Israelites put the blinder on in order to destroy their rivals the Midianites, and the Christians used the blinder again and again to slaughter Jews. The blinder of so-called divine vengeance makes murder seem like righteousness.

The idea that God would avenge all earthly sins was given an entire world of examples by the Italian poet Dante (1265–1321). In a long poem called the *Inferno*, Dante took his readers to Hell. The underworld, never before so meticulously described, becomes

in Dante's hands God's vast instrument for retribution. Everywhere one looks, sinners suffer the vengeance of God. Each particular sin is matched with a specific punishment. The lustful, who allowed their turbulent desires to rule them in life, are blown about forever by a torrential storm. Hypocrites are forced to walk unceasingly under lead capes that appear to be made of gold. Violent criminals must lie for all eternity submerged in a river of boiling blood.

Dante reflected not only the belief—widespread among common people in Christian Europe by the late Middle Ages, when the *Inferno* was written—that God would repay all sins, but also the belief that all vengeance should be left to God. One of those residing in the lowest reaches of Hell is a man named Ugolino, who made the mistake of exacting private revenge. God punishes Ugolino by freezing him into a lake

By the Middle Ages, revenge had become much less widespread in Christian Europe. But the retributive practices of medieval rulers, many of whom claimed to be enacting divine justice, were generally barbaric. In this illustration, the criminal at left is having his limbs broken by the wheel; the two convicts on the right are being boiled in oil.

beside the man he killed and forcing him to tear the man's brains out with his teeth, again and again, world without end.

If to many devout Christians during the Middle Ages the idea of divine vengeance meant that only God had the right to vengeance, to members of the nobility, it meant something entirely different. To Europe's kings, queens, and lesser nobles, divine vengeance was the justification for a host of harsh laws. The European rulers painted every act of public retribution as an act ordained by God, but the punishment of wrongdoers often had less to do with heaven than with preserving and strengthening the social and political privileges of the nobility. Thus, while private revenge was no longer as acute a problem as it had been in previous societies—though Christianity had by no means eliminated the revenge ethic—public retribution was now being used for private purposes. And public retribution had run amok.

Centuries before, in Athens, all citizens had worked together to agree upon what form justice should take in their society. Euripides had seen the danger of powerful men like Tyndareos using public retribution for their own selfish purposes. The Middle Ages unfolded like the Athenian playwright's worst nightmare. Justice degenerated into the private instrument of tyrants.

These tyrants repayed any challenge to their authority with a brutality so excessive it made the revenge of Achilles look relatively tame. While Achilles had been one man acting alone, the medieval ruler had his whole kingdom behind him. And whereas Achilles had only a sword, the medieval ruler had an entire arsenal of weapons of torture. Like Achilles, the monarchs sought to do much worse than what had been done to them. With their vast power and the ever-advancing technology of torture, they were able to make their world into a hell on earth for those unfortunate enough to cross them.

By the tail end of the Middle Ages, the vengeance of the rulers had concretized into law. An ordinance from France, typical of the times, showed just how far the Christian world had strayed from Jesus' words on the mountain in Galilee. It read:

Some prisoners may be condemned to be hanged, others to having their hands cut off or their tongues cut out or pierced and then to be hanged; others, for more serious crimes, to be broken alive and to die on the wheel, after having their limbs broken; others to be broken until they die a natural death, others to be strangled and then broken, others to be burnt alive, others to be burnt after first being strangled; others to be drawn [pulled limb from limb] by the four horses, others to have their heads cut off, and others to have their heads broken.

WAKING FROM A NIGHTMARE

Hamlet (Mel Gibson) shrinks from the apparition of his dead father, the former king of Denmark, in this scene from Franco Zeffirelli's 1990 motion-picture adaptation of Shakespeare's famous play. In the story, the ghost commands Hamlet to avenge his death by killing his murderer, Hamlet's uncle Claudius, but Hamlet hesitates.

The king and queen sweep in, their royal robes flowing, attendants trailing behind. The king gives orders and entertains requests. It seems that all is proceeding as it should, that this is a kingdom rolling along without a problem, but all the while there is the subtle feeling that something is wrong.

It's the young man in the background, dressed in black. He hasn't said anything yet, but his sullen presence ticks at the center of the scene like a time bomb. The king finally turns to this young man and asks him, "How is it that the clouds still hang on you?"

This is the first glimpse we get of the title character in William Shakespeare's play *Hamlet*. The play was written at the turn of the 17th century, a time when the many clouds produced in the Middle Ages still hung over the people of Europe. For centuries, what had passed for fair and even divine retribution had been only the savage vengeance of power-hungry rulers.

By 1600 questions that had lain dormant for centuries—since the golden age of democracy in Athens—had begun to resurface. These ancient questions would be the ones Hamlet would grapple with throughout the play: What is justice? What is the relationship between justice and vengeance? These were the questions that would have to be addressed once again if civilization was to wake from the long nightmare that the vengeful despots had authored.

By the time Shakespeare (1564–1616) wrote *Hamlet*, other playwrights had been edging toward such questions. In the 1500s, revenge plays had become immensely popular. The popularity of these dramas hinged on the fact that they involved characters who, because of the wrongful death of someone close to them, took it upon themselves to seek justice. The audience was able to imagine a situation in which an individual was involved in the search for justice.

The revenge plays marked the fact that civilization had in some ways come full circle on the question of revenge. In the beginning, private revenge had been the only form of justice. Societies had come to realize that leaving justice solely in the hands of the individual led to serious problems, and they had therefore put limitations on private revenge. But by the 1500s a new kind of injustice had become ensconced: the injustice of state-controlled retribution running amok. And now the individual was virtually shut out of the justice system. True, jury trials were conducted in England, for example, but the state had broad powers to coerce the verdicts it wanted—including the power to punish jurors for rendering an unpopular decision—and the monarch's subjects had no voice in the creation of laws. The revenge plays spoke to an awakening desire for the individual to be involved once again—directly—in the process of justice.

In *Hamlet*, the main character's dilemma begins when his dead father, the former king, appears to him

Thomas More, author of Utopia, *was among the thinkers who began questioning the harshness of their societies' retributive practices as Europe emerged from the Middle Ages.*

in the form of a ghost. He tells Hamlet that he was murdered by his own brother, Hamlet's uncle, Claudius, the man who now wears the robes of the king. He commands Hamlet to exact revenge.

In many ways obeying the Ghost is against Hamlet's nature. Unlike other characters in the play—including the usurper Claudius; Fortinbras, the warrior-king who will eventually take his kingdom; and, presumably, Hamlet's dead father—Hamlet recoils at the prospect of shedding blood, and he is not at all interested in the exercise of power. And yet he knows that there is a need for justice in his world and that he is the only one who can bring that justice to pass. He senses early on that such a burden will be a crushing one. After hearing the command of the Ghost for the first time, he says, "The time is out of joint. O, cursed spite, / That ever I was born to set it right!"

Hamlet's awakening to the fact that his world lacks justice reflected a similar awakening in European society. In the 1500s, philosophers known as the Utopians, led by a man named Thomas More (1478–1535), began questioning such things as the extreme harshness of their societies' penal codes. The philosophers attempted to envision a better world. In their attempts they began a movement toward the kind of participatory government that the ancient Athenians had briefly been able to sustain, a government in which justice was more than a blood-soaked ax wielded by a king.

Democracy had not yet reappeared at the time of Hamlet's creation, however. And so he had no one to look to but himself if he wanted to see justice done. But his awareness of the need for justice was matched by an awareness that revenge required the act of murder.

For much of the play, Hamlet is paralyzed with inaction. He knows he can't let the murder of his father go unpunished. At the same time, he struggles with the idea of taking a life in cold blood. Eventually his desire for revenge and justice overcomes his qualms about killing. But things go tragically wrong. Hamlet passes up an opportunity to kill Claudius while the king is praying because, as a Christian, he believes that Claudius's soul will go to heaven if he dies with pious thoughts. Better that the end should come when Claudius is engaged in some base act. At one point Hamlet thrusts a dagger through a curtain in his mother's bedchamber and kills a man named Polonius, mistaking him for Claudius. But face-to-face, when there is no curtain to hide the act, Hamlet hesitates.

In the play, Shakespeare creates a paradox that he leaves largely unsolved. An individual like Hamlet, who is bright enough and noble enough to see the need for justice, is also bright enough to sense that revenge includes the horrifying act of murder. If Shakespeare had lived in ancient Athens, he might have reconciled this paradox by having the goddess Athena materialize to lead a council of citizens toward a just solution. But his play ends not with reconciliation and peace but with a massacre that claims among its number the would-be bringer of justice, Hamlet.

But the questions about justice and the relationship of revenge to justice that Shakespeare raised would continue to be asked. The century after Shakespeare's death would become known as the Age of Enlightenment. Thinkers and writers in a variety of intellectual fields turned a questioning eye toward the issues of their world.

The most important of these thinkers, as far as the problem of revenge and retribution is concerned, was an Italian criminologist named Cesare Beccaria (1738–1794). To Beccaria, every act of savage state-run retribution that had become the norm over the centuries was nothing more than the thrusting of a dagger through a curtain to kill someone. It was murder, even if the rulers who ordered it never looked the person they were murdering in the eye. It was also highly irrational. Beccaria said, "To me it appears absurd that the laws . . . which detest and punish murder, should themselves commit a murder; and to deter citizens from killing, should ordain a killing in public."

Beccaria was skeptical of the state's ability to restrain its vindictive impulses. Earlier civilizations had been skeptical of a victim's ability to restrain these impulses. They were right to be wary, since it seems to be a natural human reaction to want to repay one injury with an even larger injury. The way these societies guarded against that impulse toward excess was to take the act of retribution for a crime out of the hands of the individual.

Beccaria and other Enlightenment theorists had only to take a good look around to see that the balance had swung too far in the other direction. The state itself had become like a feverishly vengeful individual, unable to control its vindictive impulses.

"If I am not myself so barbarous, so bloody-minded, and revengeful, as to kill a fellow-creature" for a minor offense, wondered Benjamin Franklin, "how can I approve of a law that does it?"

The taming of vindictive impulses had been an ongoing question of the utmost importance for human societies since the dawn of time. In the Enlightenment a huge advance toward that elusive goal was taken when certain thinkers realized that the taming of the vindictive impulse could not be achieved simply by the prohibition of private revenge. Public retribution had to have limitations put on it as well.

Beccaria called for checks on the system and for reforms on the retributive practices of the various states of Europe. He saw as the most important point that ret-ribution for a crime should be neither excessive nor trivial. There was a need to punish criminals; society's health depended on the upholding of certain guide-lines, and Beccaria was in no way promulgating the repeal of all punishments. He believed that, to be effec-tive in deterring criminal behavior, punishment had to be prompt, certain, and moderate. He felt that society was being grievously harmed by the excessive use of force—including torture and capital punishment—in public retribution.

Part of what motivated Beccaria and other Enlight-enment thinkers into seeking limits on public retribu-tion was that they saw that they were fundamentally connected to the laws their societies enforced. They were part of every inhumane punishment and every state-sponsored execution. Another great figure of the Enlightenment, the American statesman and philoso-pher Benjamin Franklin (1706–1790), articulated this new feeling of personal responsibility for the laws of a state. Upon hearing of the execution of a woman for the crime of stealing some bandages that had a paltry monetary value, Franklin said, "If I am not myself so barbarous, so bloody-minded, and revengeful, as to kill a fellow-creature for stealing from me 14 shillings and three pence, how can I approve of a law that does it?"

The first reforms in the practice of public retribu-tion were not lasting. This is because they were enact-ed by rulers who would come to be known as enlight-ened despots. These rulers, who had seen the reason of the Enlightenment thinkers, had acted on their own to change the retributive practices of their countries. The problem was, since these changes did not come about by popular demand, they were overturned as quickly as they had been instituted by less-enlightened successors to the throne.

Lasting reforms first occurred as an outgrowth of the democratic movements in America and France. It was

Swiss-born French philosopher Jean-Jacques Rousseau, whose writings influenced America's Founding Fathers, foresaw a society in which laws expressed the general will of the people.

in these places that the demands of the individual and the state were balanced as they never had been before.

Much of the political philosophy that underpinned the American Revolution came from Europe, where in the 17th and 18th centuries thinkers sought to define the conditions under which legitimate governments are constituted. These thinkers included the English philosophers Thomas Hobbes (1588–1679) and John Locke (1632–1704) and the Frenchman Jean-Jacques Rousseau (1712–1778).

Hobbes, Locke, and Rousseau explained societies and governments in light of the social contract, an agreement that spelled out the obligations of citizens to their government and of government to its citizens. Though they differed in their descriptions of some of the details, the philosophers agreed on the broad outlines of the social contract. Individuals join together to form societies and set up governments in order to protect their persons and their property, which by themselves they would not be able to do. As part of the bargain, they relinquish some of their freedom to act as individuals. Government, for its part, is obliged not to break the terms of the contract, which may be tacit or explicitly stated. According to Rousseau, that means that the government must carry out the will of the people—who are sovereign—or the people may revoke their consent to be governed. And it is by the consent of the people alone that government functions.

The relevance of social contract theory to the issue of revenge and retribution is clear. One of the freedoms members of society give up in exchange for their personal security is the freedom to pursue private justice. But at the same time, the retributive practices of a government must be in accord with the will of its citizens.

After the success of the American—and later, French—Revolution, retribution was no longer in the hands of kings who claimed they were acting out the divine vengeance of God. The kings had been over-

The United States Supreme Court, where constitutional issues such as the meaning of the Eighth Amendment's ban on cruel and unusual punishment are resolved.

thrown. For the first time in thousands of years, citizens would have a significant voice in deciding what shape justice would take.

In America, the Founding Fathers attempted to guard against excessive retribution on the part of the state. The Eighth Amendment to the Constitution, written in 1789, states, "Excessive bail shall not be required, nor excessive fines imposed, nor cruel and unusual punishments inflicted."

Over the years, the precise meaning of these words has been much debated. And, in fact, at the time the

Bill of Rights was put forward, not everyone agreed with even the general principle that the Eighth Amendment enunciated. For example, in 1789 Samuel Livermore, a congressional critic of the amendment, not only declared that the cruel and unusual punishment clause "seems to have no meaning in it" but also observed that "it is sometimes necessary to hang a man, villains often deserve whipping, and perhaps having their ears cut off; but are we in the future to be prevented from inflicting these punishments because they are cruel?"

Today one would be hard-pressed to find many Americans who seriously dispute the wisdom of prohibiting cruel and unusual punishment. However, not everyone agrees on what exactly constitutes such punishment. While perhaps the vast majority of Americans would now classify as cruel and unusual whipping or cutting off the ears of criminals—which Livermore viewed as sometimes necessary 200 years ago—there is often little consensus regarding other forms of punishment. The most prominent example is the death penalty. Polls show that a majority of Americans support capital punishment, although a substantial and vocal minority are adamantly opposed, and several former Supreme Court justices have stated that the death penalty violates the Eighth Amendment. It is highly unlikely that, 200 years ago, or even 100 years ago, any American jurist—much less a member of the Supreme Court—would have staked out such a position. But the courts have continually wrestled with the meaning of the Eighth Amendment, and as society's notions about punishment have changed, so too have judicial decisions. As Chief Justice Earl Warren wrote in a 1958 decision:

> The basic concept underlying the Eighth Amendment is nothing less than the dignity of man. While the State has the power to punish, the Amendment stands to assure that this power be exercised within the limits of civilized

standards. . . . The Court [has] recognized . . . that the words of the Amendment are not precise, and that their scope is not static. The Amendment must draw its meaning from the evolving standards of decency that mark the progress of a maturing society.

Thus, while the amendment has played a crucial role in limiting the retribution enacted by the state upon lawbreakers, changing societal values have been an equally important factor. Although in recent years there has been widespread sentiment for "getting tough" on criminals, as a general trend, punishment in the United States has become less severe. Once again, the death penalty is illustrative. One hundred thirty-five years ago, burglary and robbery were capital offenses in more than a few jurisdictions; 120 years ago, the horse thief could look forward to hanging. In this cen-

Helen Goldstone, accompanied by an assistant district attorney, arrives at court to deliver a victim-impact statement during the penalty phase in the trial of a man who shot her. Victims'-rights advocates say that allowing victims to testify about the personal impact of a crime restores to them an appropriate role in a criminal-justice system that typically shuts them out.

tury, armed robbers were sometimes sentenced to death, and, a scant 25 years ago, so too were kidnappers and rapists. Now, with certain exceptions (such as treason), the death penalty is reserved for first-degree murderers, and generally only when there is an aggravating circumstance (such as multiple murders or deliberate cruelty to the victim).

Retributive justice is a balancing act. Wrongdoers must be treated fairly and humanely, according to society's current legal and moral standards, yet citizens must also believe that the system sufficiently punishes.

A recent concern has been the perceived imbalance between the rights of criminals and the rights of their victims. According to many victims, they are, for all intents and purposes, shut out of the justice system. This has led to a movement to reclaim a role for victims. Perhaps the most prominent manifestation of the victims'-rights movement is the use of victim-impact statements, which many jurisdictions now permit. Victim-impact statements, which allow the victim of a crime or the victim's family to tell the jury about the personal impact the crime has had, are generally reserved for crimes of violence and are especially important in capital murder cases.

Typically, capital trials are conducted in two phases. During the first phase, the issue is whether or not the defendant committed the crime. If the jury decides that he or she did, the trial moves to the penalty phase, when the issue is whether the defendant should receive the death penalty or life imprisonment. The defense presents evidence of mitigating circumstances, such as a difficult childhood, and often calls family members to testify about the defendant's good character or deeds. The prosecution may call members of the victim's family to tell about the victim's life, character, goals, and dreams—as well as about the intense pain of losing a loved one. Such testimony, obviously, is emotionally wrenching, but victims'-rights advocates say that it can help people come to terms with their loss. And, perhaps more importantly, it gives victims a significant role in a retributive justice system that, in order to prevent revenge and to be fair to accused criminals, largely excludes victims.

"You Do It to Feel Strong"

On the afternoon of December 22, 1984, in New York City, four black teenagers approached a bespectacled white man sitting alone on a downtown IRT subway train. The youths surrounded the lone passenger, Bernhard Goetz, and one of them asked if he had five dollars. Goetz, who had been mugged by a group of teenagers just months before, concluded that these kids, too, were planning to rob him. But he never gave them that chance. He reached into his coat pocket and produced the .38-caliber handgun he had obtained shortly after his recent mugging. Within seconds all four of the teenagers lay bleeding on the subway floor. Goetz shot one of the youths in the back as he was running away. Walking up to the prone youth, he declared, "You don't look so bad. Have another" and, for good measure, pumped another slug into him before disappearing into the crowds of New York City.

The incident, which received abundant—and at

times, sensationalistic—news coverage, riveted the nation. But what precisely happened in that subway and why became a matter of some debate. Was Goetz a racist looking for an excuse to shoot some blacks, as some African-American commentators charged? Or did he merely feel threatened by the situation, as he confessed to the police? Were the youths going to rob him, as one of them later admitted and as might be inferred from the sharpened screwdrivers they were carrying, or were they merely panhandling, as they maintained at Goetz's trial? Was this really a case of self-defense, or was Goetz in his own mind compensating for his earlier victimization, paying someone back, just as Leif O'Connel would do a decade later in Indiana?

These questions, perhaps, will never be answered definitively. But in a certain respect, the reality of Goetz's personal psychology and the intentions of the youths who surrounded him that December afternoon are less important than the public reaction to the shootings. As the story got picked up by local and then national media in the days following the incident, the press dubbed the unknown shooter "the Subway Vigilante," and in the minds of millions of people across the country, he was an avenging hero. He was, many people imagined, like the character Dirty Harry, a tough-talking, straight-shooting San Francisco cop played by Clint Eastwood in a series of popular movies. Self-defense may have been the initial reason the Subway Vigilante had pulled his gun, but punishing a street thug was the reason he shot the kid in the back and again after he was already down.

When Bernhard Goetz surrendered to the police days later, the man the public saw didn't seem to fit the image of an avenging hero. He didn't look like Clint Eastwood or talk like Dirty Harry. Rather, he was a gangly, nervous-looking, even mouselike man who said he had felt like a cornered rat on the subway train.

But when Goetz was charged with attempted mur-

Unlikely vigilante?: Goetz in the custody of police.

der, the public rallied to his cause. New York City's mayor, Ed Koch, received an overwhelming barrage of calls and letters that had an average ratio of 80 to 1 in support of Goetz's actions.

The Goetz case became a lightning rod for a widespread voicing of dissatisfaction with the law enforcement and criminal justice system in America. Nearly 200 years before, the authors of the Constitution had attempted to lay the foundation for a just and peaceful society. It was to be a society predicated on laws that both protected the law-abiding and protected the rights of those accused of wrongdoing. Clearly, many Americans now had doubts that such a society had been created.

The public saw Goetz as someone who had stood up for himself, someone who had taken into his own hands

Actor Charles Bronson, playing a mild-mannered architect turned vigilante, prepares to dispatch a street punk in the 1974 motion picture Death Wish. *In the minds of many people, the Goetz case mirrored this popular movie.*

the too-often ineffective law—which seemed to protect criminals more than victims. He had become a vigilante, one who instantly judges a criminal case and who instantly punishes those he finds guilty. He had set aside public justice in favor of a private solution, and for that he was seen as a hero.

And that, perhaps, is the most significant aspect of the Goetz case—that many Americans seem to endorse, or at least to tolerate, private justice. An ancient problem is seen, more and more, as not a problem at all but instead as a solution.

The belief that violent crime is increasing and the spreading perception that violent offenders are not made to suffer at all for their crimes contribute mightily to this attitude. The feeling of the Enlightenment—that the retributive punishments of the state had become much too severe—has largely vanished. In its place is the contrary feeling that the state doesn't exact enough retribution on criminals, particularly violent offenders.

"I can't believe any more there is such a thing as justice in the world," says a woman whose daughter, a 20-year-old college student, was killed in a mugging. The mugger received a sentence of zero to seven years for manslaughter and was out of jail in 30 months. "I felt as though my girl was killed twice—once by that scum, and once by the judge who said, well, you only have to go to jail for a few years. They killed her memory, saying that was all her life was worth."

The effect of a loss of belief in the justice system is a grave one. Susan Jacoby, in her 1983 study of revenge titled *Wild Justice*, wrote, "A society that is unable to convince individuals of its ability to exact atonement for injury is a society that runs the constant risk of having its members revert to the wilder forms of justice."

The initial public support of Goetz is strong evidence that many people have lost faith in society's ability to exact atonement. Might we find further evidence, some people wonder, in the immense money-making ability of private revenge stories in all forms of popular culture? Public adulation of private avengers is reinforced time and time again through the popularity of movies, books, pop songs, and even comic books.

The Bernhard Goetz affair, in many ways, was simply a case of life imitating these popular myths. To the people who rallied in support of him, he was the real-life counterpart to the kind of fictional avenging angel that has become, with each passing year, a more and more popular figure in America. Through these avengers audiences can revel in their own fantasies of revenge.

The father of all the private revenge fantasy movies that have proliferated at an ever-increasing rate in the last two decades is the 1974 movie *Death Wish*. It was this movie that, in the eyes of many, the case of Bernhard Goetz most closely resembled. In it Charles Bronson plays a liberal-minded architect who changes his view of the world after his wife is killed in a robbery.

The critical turning point for Bronson's character comes when he sees that there is little, if any, chance that his wife's killers will be brought to justice. He then decides to take matters into his own hands, cruising through crime-infested areas of New York City (which is depicted as a human cesspool teeming on every street corner with out-of-control crime and violence) while packing a large, Lone Ranger–style pistol.

Susan Jacoby described the kind of reaction that the popular movie got in packed movie houses across the country: "The audience cheered each time he pulled out his gun and dispatched yet another teenager who gave him a shifty glance or walked with an aggressive swagger."

Viewed today, *Death Wish* may seem almost tame. After its explosive success, movie companies began churning out revenge fantasy stories, and over the years these stories have escalated in their levels of violence. The kind of character that Bronson played—someone who at least outwardly resembles a regular person—was abandoned for muscle-bound, grenade-launching supermen capable of channeling their urges for revenge into the annihilation, if need be, of entire worlds. Arnold Schwarzenegger's 1986 movie *Raw Deal* was advertised by a poster that featured the thick-tongued thespian wrapped in various firearms and explosive devices, his gigantic chest muscles rippling beneath

them. Across the top of the movie poster was written a slogan that made the theme of the movie quite clear: "Somewhere. Somehow. Someone is going to pay." In another revenge fantasy from the previous year, a run-away box-office hit entitled *Rambo: First Blood II*, a bulging Sylvester Stallone, toting an automatic weapon the size of a small tree, personally avenges America's defeat in the Vietnam War by slicing scores of Viet-namese foes to ribbons.

The revenge fantasy, as enacted by these grunting, monosyllabic muscle men, became even more problem-free than it had been in *Death Wish*. In *Death Wish*, there had at least been the ghost of a hint that the main character was perhaps veering toward a kind of mental

"You do it to feel strong": The code of blood-vengeance flourishes today among the street gangs of the nation's cities.

state a little beyond perfect sanity. Of course, such hints were lost in the roar of the crowd that approved every act of violence Bronson engaged in. Apparently, moviemakers sensed that calling an avenger's sanity into question, much less calling the act of private revenge itself into question, was something that needn't be done to make a killing on ticket sales. *Rambo* and *Raw Deal* were two examples among many movies that had no trace of a question about the legitimacy of private justice, including revenge.

The ambivalence toward revenge that Hamlet had exhibited, centuries before, was nowhere to be seen in any of these movies. More than any other character in history, Hamlet had sensed that a fatal act of private revenge equals murder, and he questioned whether the act of revenge was right or wrong with his entire being. In the midst of all the gunfire and explosions of contemporary stories, it seems, that questioning spirit has been lost. And yet, whether this—or, for that matter, support for Bernhard Goetz—in itself signifies that a substantial number of Americans are themselves willing to resort to private justice is debatable. Revenge fantasies are, after all, fantasies.

What is undeniable is that right now, in certain pockets of America, the ancient practice of blood-vengeance serves as the predominant form of justice. In the gang wars that rage in the poor sections of cities from coast to coast, there is the kind of wild payback that was seen in the earliest, most brutal societies. One death is avenged by 10 deaths. Corpses are stolen from funeral homes so the bodies can be further mutilated. Those who prove to be adept at the blood-vengeance of street gangs are treated with the utmost respect. They are warriors. They are heroes.

A native of South Central Los Angeles named Kody Scott wanted to be one of these heroes since he was a young boy. Later, he came to the realization that he had been attracted to the life of a gangster because it was the only way he could see that would allow him to go about forming an identity. By entering the bloody world of paying back one injury with an even greater injury, Kody Scott found a way toward a kind of honor and renown: he became known as Monster, his nickname a testament to his ability to give back worse than he received.

In his autobiography, written in prison, he describes the moment when, at the age of 15, he fully entered the culture of blood-vengeance: "I had been to five funerals in the previous two years and had been steeled by seeing people whom I had laughed with and joked with, played and eaten with, dead in a casket. Revenge was my every thought."

In Monster's world, there is no faith whatsoever that the American justice system will exact atonement for an injury. The America the Founding Fathers envisioned has nothing to do with Monster's world. In that world, a person either has to stand up for himself or get trampled. Revenge is a way to stand up.

Thousands of years before, Euripides had noted this aspect of revenge when he had the vengeful heroine of the play *Medea* proclaim, "Let no one think of me as humble or weak or passive; let them understand I am dangerous to my enemies, loyal to my friends. To such a life glory belongs."

The blood-vengeance of the nation's gangbangers is fueled by the desire to send out Medea's message loud and clear. A gang member from Los Angeles named James B. explained why he and his fellow members banded together to strike back at their rivals: "You do it out of togetherness. You do it to feel strong."

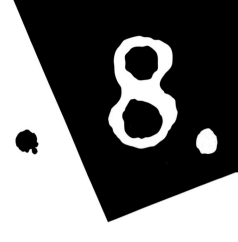

MIRROR, MIRROR

Steven Seagal in a scene from the motion picture Hard to Kill, *which depicted the main character's quest to avenge the murder of his family. What, some people wonder, does the popularity of this and other revenge fantasies say about Americans' faith in the justice system?*

Leon is 17 years old and lives in the same kind of world Monster grew up in. Writing poems makes him feel strong. His poems have a heartbeat. The heartbeat rips like gunfire sometimes, and sometimes flutters like angel wings. He sees the world he lives in, a rundown section of a big American city, streets with too much violent crime, too much sorrow, too little justice. He also tries to see a better world.

One day he's walking home and four other teenagers beat him, take his wallet, and leave him bleeding on the street. Every bone in his body aches. He limps home and looks in the mirror. His face is covered with bumps and blood. His eyes are blackened. His lips are swollen. He spits in the sink and his spit is crimson.

He wants to go wild on those who did this to him. They outnumber him, but in this world that's not a problem. It's not a problem in the movies. It's not a problem in the streets. People take revenge all the time. They get their hands on a gun and give back worse than they got. It's the way things are done, and Leon wants to do it that way. He wants revenge.

He's looking in the mirror, thinking only about doing some damage, when a tiny light comes on in his mind. He sees past the payback he's planning to a time when he's once again looking at his reflection. What would he see if he took revenge? "I'd be looking in the mirror," he says. "I'd be seeing them instead of myself."

What would you see if you took revenge?

In America, this question is being asked less and less. The damage revenge can do is not often considered. Wild vengeance thrives in pop culture fantasies and on city streets. And, some might argue, the vindictive impulse has also found a home in the nation's laws.

Among industrialized Western democracies, the United States stands alone in retaining the death penalty. Forty-five convicts were executed in the United States in 1996; that number increased significantly in 1997, when 74 were put to death.

Between 1967 and 1972, opponents of capital punishment raised constitutional objections to the death penalty, arguing that it violated the Eighth Amendment's ban on cruel and unusual punishment and the Fourteenth Amendment's "due process" clause. Absent a Supreme Court decision on the issues, executions in the United States were suspended. In January 1972, the Court heard the case of *Furman v. Georgia,* in which a black man had been sentenced to die for killing a white man during a robbery, despite the fact that his gun had gone off accidentally when he tripped while running away, and despite the fact that the bullet had passed through a closed door before striking the victim in the chest. In a 5-4 decision delivered in June of 1972, the Court ruled that America's death-penalty statutes as written were cruel and unusual because they permitted death sentences to be handed out arbitrarily. Wrote Justice Potter Stewart:

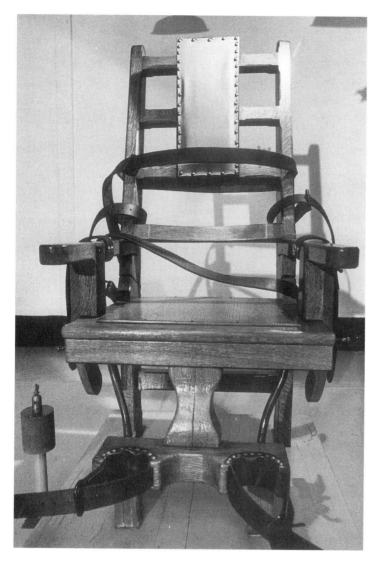

As more and more countries abolish the death penalty, executions in the United States are on the rise. Is the electric chair an example of excessive state retribution? According to opinion polls, a majority of Americans don't think so.

The death sentences are cruel and unusual in the same way that being struck by lightning is cruel and unusual. . . . [T]he [Eighth Amendment] cannot tolerate the infliction of a sentence of death under legal systems that permit this unique penalty to be so wantonly and freakishly imposed.

With the Supreme Court's *Furman* decision, all of the country's death-penalty statutes were invalidated.

"The instinct for retribution is part of the nature of man," wrote Supreme Court justice Potter Stewart (at right), *"and channeling that instinct in the administration of criminal justice serves an important purpose in promoting the stability of a society governed by law."*

But that didn't necessarily mean that the Court believed differently written statutes could not pass constitutional muster. In 1976 the Court heard another key death-penalty case, *Gregg v. Georgia*. Gregg had been condemned to die for a double murder. His lawyers argued, among other things, that however it was imposed and for whatever crime, the death penalty was cruel and unusual and therefore unconstitutional. The Constitution had been based in large part, after all, on the Enlightenment-era thinking of such men as Cesare Beccaria. The Supreme Court rejected the argument, ruling in favor of what Beccaria would have seen as state-sanctioned murder.

Since then, 38 states have instituted death-penalty statutes. And popular opinion seems firmly in support of this fatal form of public retribution. In a 1996 Gallup poll, for example, 79 percent said they favored the death penalty. (An earlier poll, however, found that only 50 percent favored the death penalty if life imprisonment without parole was offered as an option.)

Those in support of the death penalty argue that the severe penalty will make potential criminals think twice before committing a heinous crime. Opponents of the policy respond by pointing to statistics that show violent crime rates to be unaffected by the institution of the death penalty.

But arguments over whether or not the penalty is a deterrent do not cut to the heart of the matter. The real argument concerns whether or not the state has a right to kill.

Supreme Court justice Potter Stewart, who four years earlier had objected to the "wanton and freakish" way the death penalty was imposed, was among those who ruled in favor of the death penalty in 1976. Stewart believed that the state needs to reserve the right to exact the severest form of retribution to keep wilder forms of justice in check. He wrote, "The instinct for retribution is part of the nature of man, and channeling that instinct in the administration of criminal justice serves an important purpose in promoting the stability of a society governed by law."

If the state did not satisfy the ancient urge to repay blood with blood, Stewart believed, then private acts of revenge would increase in a blind, general clawing for justice. We would veer toward a culture of blood-vengeance, the same kind of violent world that, thousands of years before, lawmakers and visionaries had attempted again and again to bring to an end.

Critics of the death penalty echo Cesare Beccaria's beliefs, wondering how a state that condemns murder can itself commit murder. They see the death penalty as a vestige of a time before the Age of Enlightenment, a time when public retribution ran as wild as any kind of private revenge ever has. The memory of the gallows of the Middle Ages hovers like a ghost over the modern-day practice of putting a criminal to death.

The modern practices of fatal public retribution are carried out in a much less gory—and much less public—way than their medieval ancestors. This is done in large part, critics charge, to support the claim that the death penalty is a rational act, carried out beyond the reach of volatile emotions.

Prison warden Don Cabana offers another view of the death penalty. He presided over the execution of a convict named Edward Earl Johnson. "Afterward," says Cabana, "I felt dirty. I remember standing in the shower at three o'clock in the morning, scrubbing as hard as I could. No matter what I tried, nothing seemed to put my mind at ease.

"The rest of the world could afford to be matter-of-fact. I thought, they had not strapped a man into a chair and killed him. I would remember every detail about Edward Earl Johnson—every wrinkle, every blemish—forever."

The authors of the Constitution and the Bill of Rights strove to put the power for determining what shape justice takes in our society in the hands of the citizens. An act of public retribution in America is an act sanctioned by the American people. If the state puts someone to death, everyone straps that person into the chair and kills him.

"The thirst for vengeance," Supreme Court justice Benjamin Cardozo wrote, "is a very real, even if it be a hideous, thing; and states may not ignore it till humanity has been raised to greater heights than any that have yet been scaled in all the long ages of struggle and ascent."

Until the day comes when humanity reaches those heights, the question we, as a society, must continually ask is this: When we look in the mirror, do we like what we see?

Further Reading

Barreca, Regina. *Sweet Revenge*. New York: Harmony Books, 1995.

Foucault, Michel. *Discipline and Punish: The Birth of the Prison*. New York: Pantheon Books, 1977.

Jacoby, Susan. *Wild Justice*. New York: Harper and Row, 1983.

Kerrigan, John. *Revenge Tragedy: Aeschylus to Armageddon*. Oxford: Clarendon Press, 1996.

Marongiu, Pierre, and Graeme Newman. *Vengeance*. Totowa, N.J.: Rowman and Littlefield Publishers, 1987.

Scott, Kody. *Monster: The Autobiography of an L.A. Gang Member*. New York: Penguin, 1993.

Shakespeare, William. *Hamlet*. New York: Penguin Books, 1980.

Treston, Hubert. *Poine: A Study in Ancient Greek Blood-Vengeance*. London: Longmans, Green and Co., 1923.

Tucker, William. *Vigilante*. New York: Stein and Day, 1988.

Wekesser, Carol, ed. *The Death Penalty: Opposing Viewpoints*. San Diego: Greenhaven Press, Inc., 1991.

Index

JOSH WILKER has written several nonfiction books for young adults, most recently a biography of Confucius. He lives in Brooklyn, N.Y.

AUSTIN SARAT is William Nelson Cromwell Professor of Jurisprudence and Political Science at Amherst College, where he also chairs the Department of Law, Jurisprudence and Social Thought. Professor Sarat is the author or editor of 23 books and numerous scholarly articles. Among his books are *Law's Violence, Sitting in Judgment: Sentencing the White Collar Criminal*, and *Justice and Injustice in Law and Legal Theory*. He has received many academic awards and held several prestigious fellowships. He is currently President-Elect of the Law & Society Association and Chair of the Working Group on Law, Culture and the Humanities. In addition, he is a nationally recognized teacher and educator whose teaching has been featured in the *New York Times*, on the *Today* show, and on National Public Radio's *Fresh Air*.

Picture Credits